DISCOVERING AMERICAN INDIANS

Richard Platt

Illustrated by Luigi Galante, Manuela Cappon and Andrea Orani

ReD
KiTE

Aclnowledgements

With grateful thanks to our consultant on the book, Dr Cesare Marino,
Handbook of North American Indians, Smithsonian Institution, Washington.

We are indebted to the work of John C. Ewers and Raymond J. DeMallie for the list of buffalo products on page 11.

First published in the UK in 2005 by Red Kite Books,
an imprint of Haldane Mason Ltd
PO Box 34196, London NW10 3YB
info@haldanemason.com

Copyright © Haldane Mason Ltd, 2005

All rights reserved. No part of this publication may be reproduced,
stored in a retrieval system, or transmitted in any form or by any means,
electronic, mechanical, photocopying, recording, or otherwise, without
the prior permission of the copyright holder.

ISBN 1-902463-67-6 (with headdress)
ISBN 1-902463-69-2 (without headdress)

1 3 5 7 9 8 6 4 2

A HALDANE MASON BOOK
Art Director : Ron Samuel
All original artwork : Luigi Galante, Manuela Cappon and Andrea Orani

Colour reproduction by Universal Graphics Pte Ltd

Printed in China

Contents

Who Were the Indians?

North America's 500 tribes of native people spread across the continent from the icy Arctic to the southern deserts. As hunters, farmers and fishermen, these American Indians got all they needed from the land, lakes and seas.

Say 'American Indian' and most of us think of a painted warrior on a horse. He lives in a tipi (pronounced 'teepee'), uses a rifle to hunt buffalo, and is constantly at war with neighbouring tribes. Or perhaps we think of a leather-coated family paddling across a still lake in a bark canoe, beaching it at the foot of a totem pole. Or maybe a wily chief in a feather head-dress, sending smoke signals from a towering rock platform.

Though some of these ideas of Indian life are at least partly true, none is accurate or complete. So what were Indians really like, and how did they live? There is no simple answer, because there were many different kinds of Indians. For example, some of the Indians who lived in the scorching deserts of the Southwest were farmers, growing

▲ **Northwest life:** America's forested Pacific coast was not like the Plains, so Indians in each place lived differently. Instead of tipis, Northwest Indians had wood houses. Fishing took the place of buffalo hunts.

grain to feed themselves. Their brick houses had thick walls to protect them against the heat.

Native Americans from the damp, mountainous Northwest Coast did not need to farm. Instead, they lived on the fish that were easy to catch in the rivers and the shallow coastal waters. They also hunted game in the tall forests near the shore.

People in the frozen North built homes of snow blocks. They dressed in furs and skins, and lived by fishing and hunting caribou and seals.

Across America's rolling Plains
   A band of native Indians roams.
The land is theirs, and it provides
   All that they need — food, clothes and homes.
Hunting imaginary bears
   'Fearless Wolf' is on the prowl.
His cunning stalking brings him praise
   From his father, Silent Owl.

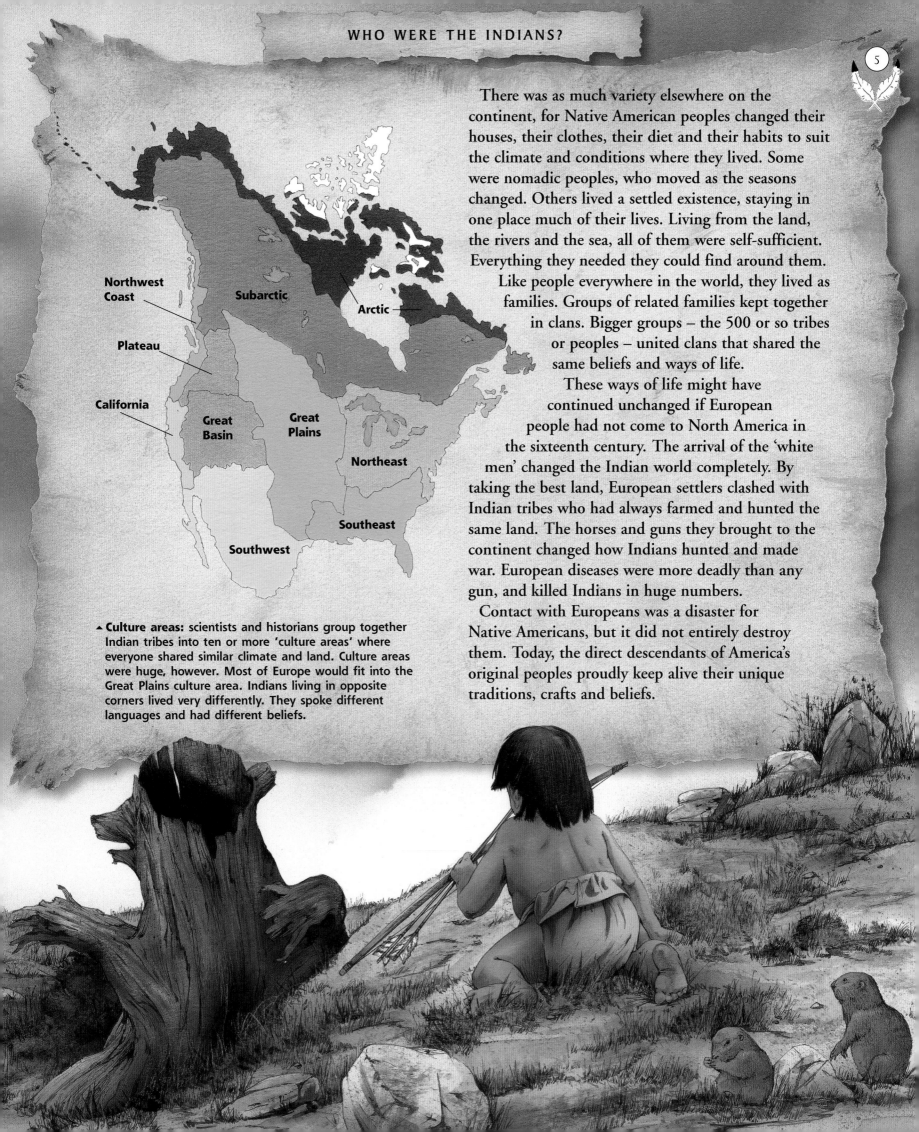

There was as much variety elsewhere on the continent, for Native American peoples changed their houses, their clothes, their diet and their habits to suit the climate and conditions where they lived. Some were nomadic peoples, who moved as the seasons changed. Others lived a settled existence, staying in one place much of their lives. Living from the land, the rivers and the sea, all of them were self-sufficient. Everything they needed they could find around them.

Like people everywhere in the world, they lived as families. Groups of related families kept together in clans. Bigger groups – the 500 or so tribes or peoples – united clans that shared the same beliefs and ways of life.

These ways of life might have continued unchanged if European people had not come to North America in the sixteenth century. The arrival of the 'white men' changed the Indian world completely. By taking the best land, European settlers clashed with Indian tribes who had always farmed and hunted the same land. The horses and guns they brought to the continent changed how Indians hunted and made war. European diseases were more deadly than any gun, and killed Indians in huge numbers.

Contact with Europeans was a disaster for Native Americans, but it did not entirely destroy them. Today, the direct descendants of America's original peoples proudly keep alive their unique traditions, crafts and beliefs.

Northwest Coast

Subarctic

Arctic

Plateau

California

Great Basin

Great Plains

Northeast

Southeast

Southwest

▲ **Culture areas:** scientists and historians group together Indian tribes into ten or more 'culture areas' where everyone shared similar climate and land. Culture areas were huge, however. Most of Europe would fit into the Great Plains culture area. Indians living in opposite corners lived very differently. They spoke different languages and had different beliefs.

Shelter

'Home' for an Indian could mean a house of rock, ice, leather or timber. The solid homes of settled peoples stood for many years on the same spot, but wandering tribes needed homes they could move easily and put up quickly.

Ice igloos, leather tipis or earthlodges do not sound comfortable or cosy compared to a modern home of brick, stone or timber. These Indian homes had many advantages, however. They were built to suit the local climate. They were made from materials that were easy to find. And because the Indians built their own houses, the shapes and structures could be adapted easily to suit the way they lived.

The most famous of Indian dwellings, the tipi (pronounced 'teepee'), was home for the Plains Indians. It was built from straight wooden poles, with a covering of stitched-together buffalo hide. It took as many as 20 skins to cover the conical wooden frame completely. A skilled Indian woman could put up a tipi in less than an hour. Large dogs or horses transported the poles and cover from place to place. An air vent at the top kept these shelters cool in summer, and a fire inside warmed them in winter.

Some Plains peoples spent the winter in more solid dwellings made in many different patterns: earthlodges, for example, were made from a frame of logs, often built around a shallow pit in the ground. Earth or turf was used to complete the walls and a dome-shaped roof.

Not all nomadic (wandering) Indian peoples used such solid shelters. Inuit people in the Arctic crafted igloos from blocks of the only material they had plenty of – frozen snow. Others improvised shelters, such as the dome-shaped wigwam, using brushwood with a covering of branches or skins.

Tribes that settled in one place for many years created much more solid, lasting homes. In the Southwest, people built superbly

As he grows older, Fearless Wolf
Feels he's different from the others.
They treat him like a foreigner,
But with each other they're like brothers.
He watches as the women build
A new earthlodge from poles, turf and mud.
The boys shout out: 'You're not like us!'
Their blows and missiles draw his blood.

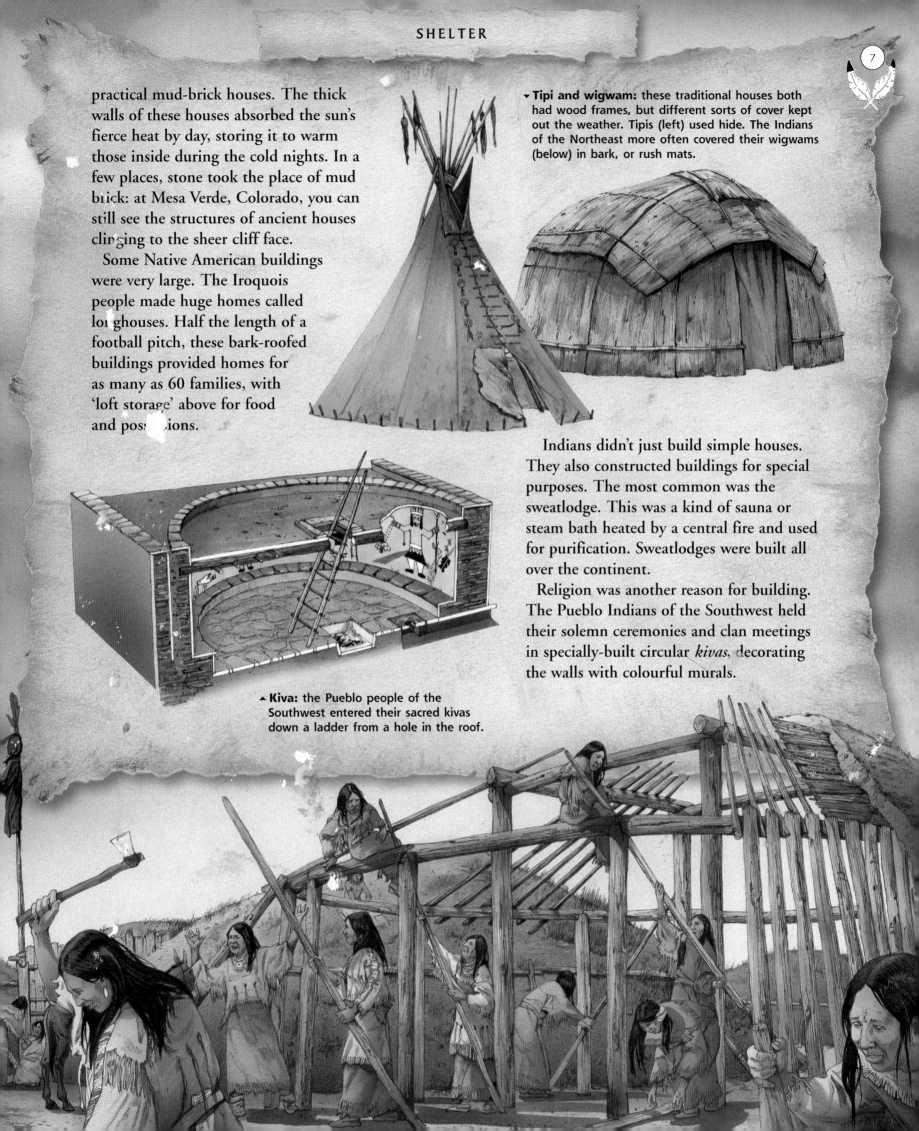

practical mud-brick houses. The thick walls of these houses absorbed the sun's fierce heat by day, storing it to warm those inside during the cold nights. In a few places, stone took the place of mud brick: at Mesa Verde, Colorado, you can still see the structures of ancient houses clinging to the sheer cliff face.

Some Native American buildings were very large. The Iroquois people made huge homes called longhouses. Half the length of a football pitch, these bark-roofed buildings provided homes for as many as 60 families, with 'loft storage' above for food and possessions.

▾ **Tipi and wigwam:** these traditional houses both had wood frames, but different sorts of cover kept out the weather. Tipis (left) used hide. The Indians of the Northeast more often covered their wigwams (below) in bark, or rush mats.

▲ **Kiva:** the Pueblo people of the Southwest entered their sacred kivas down a ladder from a hole in the roof.

Indians didn't just build simple houses. They also constructed buildings for special purposes. The most common was the sweatlodge. This was a kind of sauna or steam bath heated by a central fire and used for purification. Sweatlodges were built all over the continent.

Religion was another reason for building. The Pueblo Indians of the Southwest held their solemn ceremonies and clan meetings in specially-built circular *kivas*, decorating the walls with colourful murals.

8

I'm Hungry!

To keep hunger away, American Indians ate whatever they could find and catch, including meat, seeds, berries and fish. Though hunting was a special part of life for most Indians, many were also farmers and grew some food.

The earliest peoples of North America were hunters. Finding food was easy for them, because enormous herds of big mammals, such as mammoths (a kind of huge, hairy elephant), buffalo and musk oxen roamed the continent. A single mammoth provided food for many people. These huge beasts were dangerous, so hunters joined together to drive them over cliffs or into traps.

Mammoths and some other big game (hunt animals) were driven to extinction by the warming

Hunting

Hunters disguised in animal furs followed food animals such as deer and buffalo on foot. They crept up quietly until they were close enough to kill or wound a beast with a spear or with an arrow tipped with a stone chipped into a razor-sharp point. They skinned and butchered the kill on the spot, and divided up the carcass to carry it home.

Hunting was so important to survival that it became a central part of Indian beliefs. Many of their ceremonies aimed to guarantee success in the hunt, or celebrated a plentiful kill.

▲ **Deer trap:** hunting was hard work. A hunter band of between five and ten men had to kill four deer or one elk each day to feed a hungry tribe.

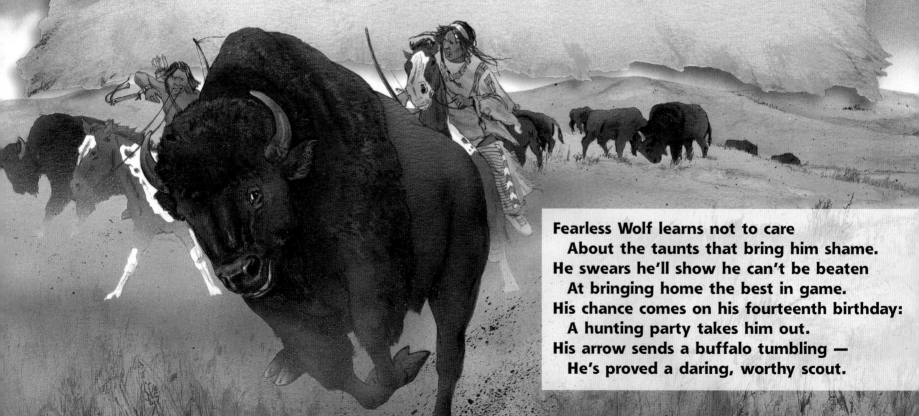

Fearless Wolf learns not to care
  About the taunts that bring him shame.
He swears he'll show he can't be beaten
  At bringing home the best in game.
His chance comes on his fourteenth birthday:
  A hunting party takes him out.
His arrow sends a buffalo tumbling —
  He's proved a daring, worthy scout.

climate, and possibly also by over-hunting (see page 11). Then America's native people were forced to become more clever to get food.

Hunters turned to stalking individual beasts rather than following whole herds. Game was small and scarce between the Pacific Ocean and the Rocky Mountains (the tall spine of peaks that runs down the continent's west side). So here people added to their diet by collecting wild plants which they had learned were good to eat. Fish were important, too, especially on the Northwest Coast, and in the Southeast, around the Gulf of Mexico. Fishermen and women used spears, traps, nets and hooks to catch fish in the sea and in lakes and rivers inland.

Some 4,000 years ago a revolution in food began: Indians in the south of the continent became farmers. When they harvested the ripe plants, they saved some of the seeds to plant the following year. The plants they grew were mostly maize (Indian corn) and beans. By the time the Europeans came

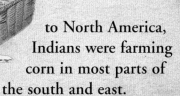

▼ **Crop plants:** although maize was the most common food plant, Native American people also grew beans and squash. Hunger was not the only reason for farming. Cotton, tobacco, herbs and dye plants all made useful crops.

to North America, Indians were farming corn in most parts of the south and east.

Despite the importance of fishing, farming and collecting, hunting remained the main source of food for many clans. However, hunting had a major drawback – unsuccessful hunts meant everyone went hungry. To help avoid famine, women preserved food in times of plenty. They dried meat in strips to make *jerky*. They also made *pemmican* by pounding meat and mixing in fat, bone marrow and berries. Pemmican lasted for up to two years.

10

Close to Nature

The Indian way of life relied completely on nature. When the plants and animals flourished, so did the people that depended on them. If the wildlife died through drought, storms, flood or frost, then human lives were lost too.

Native Americans knew how closely their lives were linked to those of the plants and animals around them. They believed that there were many ways in which they could help wildlife to flourish. Some of the steps they took were close to prayer or superstition, but other actions were similar to what we would now call 'conservation'.

The most important Indian conservation skill was their careful study of the natural world itself. They collected knowledge about how, when and where food plants grew. They watched the game, noting what animals ate, where they gathered, and how their numbers increased or fell.

▲ **Burning:** setting fires to burn shrubs and trees not only improved grazing; it also encouraged wild food plants such as berries.

This knowledge enabled them to follow the great herds of buffalo as they crossed the Plains in search of the best grazing. It helped the peoples of the Northwest to predict when the rivers would be so full of salmon that the fish could be plucked from the air as they leaped over rapids. Knowledge of nature also ensured that game numbers did not suddenly drop. Hunting families spread out across wide areas to conserve scarce game. Whole tribes came together only in seasons of plenty, when there was enough food for a big gathering.

Indian use of the natural world did not stop at hunting and fishing. They also changed the

The hunters all return at daybreak,
    Their horses carry meat and hides.
There's celebration and prayers of thanks
    For everything the hunt provides.
The skins will make fine winter clothing,
    Ropes and buckets, shields and shoes.
Hair, horns and bones are also saved
    For making things the Indians use.

Bountiful Buffalo

Finding or growing food was hard work, and took up much of the time of the adults in a clan. So it's hardly surprising that they tried to use every part of the beasts they killed. Every part of the buffalo had a use, ranging from food to shields, clothes and homes. The bits of the buffalo that were eaten included the meat, blood and bone marrow, the tongue, and the intestines, liver and other innards. Mmmmm. Other uses are shown here.

Hide: tanned hide was used for tipi covers, shoes and clothing, bags, belts, mittens and caps, bedding, dolls and as a trade item. Untanned hide was used for saddles and bridles, drums and rattles, containers and sheaths, boats, masks, bindings and snowshoes.

Tail: medicine switch, fly brush, whips and ornaments.

Dung: fuel and ceremonial smoking.

Hooves, feet: glue and rattles.

Brain: tanning the hide (to turn it into leather).

Horns: cups, spoons and ladles, fire carriers and powder flasks, toys, head-dresses, rattles.

Hair: head-dresses, padding and stuffing, ropes, halters and ornaments.

Bones: arrowheads and knives, tool handles and tools such as shovels and hoes, sled runners and saddles, paintbrushes, game counters and ceremonial objects.

Sinew: thread, bow backings, bowstrings and bindings.

countryside itself to encourage useful plants and animals. Farming peoples hoed their fields to kill weeds, which ensured that the seeds they planted grew well. Plains Indians changed the environment on a bigger scale. They lit fires to burn off trees and shrubs, preventing the rich grassland which attracted grazing buffalo from being smothered by forest.

Indian life was often a feast or a famine, though shortages were more usual. When Native American people found themselves hungry, they turned to traditions and religion for help. For example, it was a Cree habit to burn the skins of white rabbits. The winter hunts of the Cree people took place in snow, which bogged down large animals, making them easy prey for Indians wearing snowshoes (*see page* 16). Without snow, the animals escaped. The Cree believed that destroying rabbit skins would anger the rabbits' friend, the winter god, who would throw down snow as a punishment.

Crafts

Fortunate or important Indians might own a lot of beautiful, finely-crafted objects, but there was much more to wealth than the quantity or quality of someone's possessions. Skills, knowledge or sheer magical power were just as important.

Most Indian people owned little more than they needed to stay alive: their homes, clothes, weapons and tools. They made them from a huge variety of natural materials, including timber, bone, shell, stone, pottery, animal hide and cotton. Though they chose materials carefully according to what they were making, they usually crafted things from whatever was most widely available. The Nipmuck, who lived in the forests of the Northeast, made their finely-crafted bowls out of wood. But the Zuni and Anasazi of the Southwest, where few trees grow, became famous for beautifully decorated pots of clay. The Lakota Sioux hunted huge herds of buffalo on the Plains, making their hides into clothes. They added colourful decoration using the dyed quills (spines) of the porcupine.

▲ **Crafts:** the beautiful decorations on Indian crafts had a practical purpose. Signs and patterns had a magical power to protect the owner, or to bring good fortune.

Many everyday possessions were plain, and created in traditional shapes that their makers knew worked well. Their efficiency and craftsmanship gave them natural beauty. For example, Pomo women from California wove willow, rush and sedge baskets so tightly that the baskets could be filled with water. Throwing in fire-heated rocks turned the baskets into cooking pots. Often, though, the work that went into everyday articles was far greater than what was needed for them to do their job. These lovely objects became works of art.

Medicine Bundles

Among the Plains Indians, no possession was more highly valued than a medicine bundle. This was a collection of magic objects used for healing or in rituals (special sacred ceremonies). Sometimes individual people following the directions of a spirit collected the objects. But many of these magic bundles were owned by a family or a tribe. Their power came from the part they played in the myths and traditions of the group. So powerful was the magic of the medicine bundle that even opening one was a special occasion: to open their Sacred Arrows bundle took the Cheyenne four days of ceremonies.

▸ **Pipe bundle:** the contents of a medicine bundle may not look like anything special to us today. But the tobacco pipes, claws, bones, hair, fur and feathers were important because everyone believed they were powerful.

Owning beautiful and rare things was a sign of wealth, but for Indian people, being rich was not as simple as it is for us today. Some of the fine objects they 'owned' belonged not to one individual, but to a family, clan or tribe. They created many of the most beautiful things for special events, such as costumes for ceremonies or dances. Also, it wasn't just *objects* that made people wealthy. Knowledge, such as a special song

to be sung when chipping flint arrows, was as valuable as anything you could touch or handle.

Counting possessions was an unreliable way to measure wealth, because ownership depended on how people lived. Wandering people such as the Plains Indians were constantly on the move, so they kept their belongings to a minimum. But peoples who lived in fixed villages could collect more, as they did not have to carry their things around.

A sudden flood engulfs the village,
  Rushing through a family's home.
To save their precious medicine bundle,
  Their son dives in the boiling foam.
The current sweeps him down the river
  But Fearless Wolf runs along the banks.
He saves the boy from certain death,
  But hardly gets a word of thanks.

Family Life

Indian children learned from older relations the skills they would need as adults to keep themselves and their families alive. Tales, songs, prayers and legends taught them about their place in the clan and tribe.

Native American children didn't go to school, but some of them began learning before they could even speak. Along the Northwest Coast, teaching began in the cradle. Babies were rocked to sleep with folk tales. The mythical characters in them were rewarded for good behaviour, and punished for being wicked. As they grew older, children understood that these stories were really guides to what they should or should not do. Songs and prayers also helped prepare them for adult life.

For teachers, children had not only their parents, but also grandparents, uncles and aunts. They never needed lessons as we understand them. Instead they learned practical skills, customs, habits and behaviour by watching what older people did. Play was an important part of education, too. Plains children were given toy bows and blunt arrows when very young. As they grew, the bows got bigger, and the arrows sharper.

Which practical skills children learned depended on how their clan divided work between men and women. Some tribes shared most tasks, but in others the jobs were divided. The Hopi of the American

▲ **Salmon fishing:** each spring, when the salmon returned from the sea to the rivers of the Northwest, fishing was child's play. There were so many fish that it was easy to spear them, or catch them in mid-air as they leaped.

Silent Owl says: 'Now you're older,
  I'll explain why you're rejected.
You're not from this tribe, you see:
  That's why you've never been respected.
A raiding party captured you,
  Your mother too — she died soon after.
And though we raised you like a son,
  We couldn't stop the taunts and laughter.'

Southwest gave their sons jobs that required strength. Hopi daughters cooked and looked after younger brothers and sisters. Plains Indians did the same, encouraging sons to compete and fight, while their sisters made leather with their mothers.

As they grew older, children began to understand more about the structure of Indian life, and how they and their families fitted into it. In some communities everyone was equal: the Nlaka'pamux (or Thompson Indians) of the Plateau region in modern British Columbia made all important decisions in clan meetings that everyone attended. Most groups, though, had chiefs who made the big decisions. Often this important job was passed on from parent to child, but not always. The Yuma of the Southwest chose as chief the wisest and most powerful person in the clan. Other groups picked the oldest person. The chief was usually a man, but the Californian Pomo also had women chiefs.

There was great variety, too, in how people traced their family. Some families passed on their property from mother to daughter, in others, from father to son. Men were not always the family heads – among the Hopi, women were in charge. Even where fathers were supposed to be heads of the family, real life could be different. For when the men went hunting, their wives took control of the village.

Coming-of-age rituals

There were special rituals for 'firsts' in a child's life, such as the first tooth, or first game killed. Most kids also had an important 'coming-of-age' ritual that marked the change from child to adult. Girls, for instance, lived apart from the rest of the group for a time. There were ceremonies, too, for naming children. Some tribes named people more than once: Blackfoot boys had silly names, and got proper names only when they grew up.

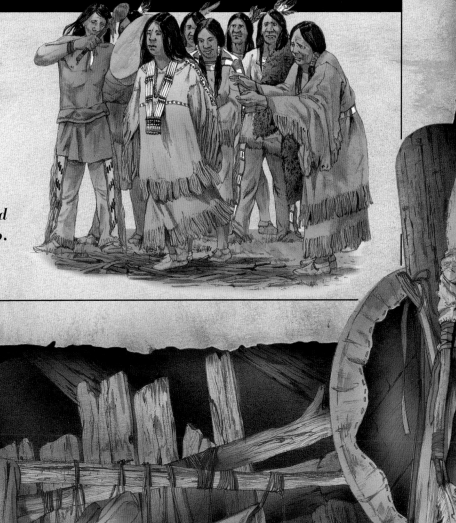

▸ **Coming of age:** Apache ritual for a young girl.

Getting Around

Before European settlers introduced horses to North America, native people used dogs, boats, sledges and snowshoes to get about. Walking and running, they created a network of tracks on routes that the modern highway system still follows.

For most Indian peoples, land transport meant putting one foot in front of the other. They travelled great distances in search of the best hunting, or to exchange goods with distant tribes. To move their possessions and young children, wandering peoples adapted a variety of containers and packs. Babies travelled in cradleboards and in pouches or parka-hoods. Tump-lines (straps supported on the forehead) and back-packs spread the weight of possessions carried in baskets, bundles and sacks.

Lacking both wheels and horses, Plains Indians had only one way to take the weight off their feet. They used dogs to carry their luggage, loading it on to a platform between two poles tied in a V called a *travois* (from the French word *travail*, meaning work). When horses came to the Plains, the travois was enlarged to carry bigger, heavier loads.

◄ Cradleboard: to transport their babies, Indian women strapped them tightly into cradleboards and carried them on their backs. A padded lining of dry moss also made a convenient disposable nappy.

▼ Travois: though it looks crude and lacks wheels, the travois made travel much easier for the Plains Indians who used it. A dog could pull a travois loaded with up to 38 kg (85 pounds) – about the weight of an 11-year-old child.

◄ Snowshoes: In snow that was too deep and soft for a sledge, snowshoes made walking easier. Tied to the feet with rawhide straps, these wooden frames spread the wearer's weight over the snow. Aided by snowshoes, Indian hunters could easily run down heavy animals that wallowed helpless in deep drifts.

Boats and canoes

Like ice, water took the work
out of travelling. There
were countless
different styles of boat,
but most were made in one
of three ways. Cutting and
burning the wood from the
middle of a log created a dugout.
These craft could be built up to
15 m (50 feet) long, and could safely
carry their crews on the open ocean. They
were especially popular in the Northwest.
Dugouts had one major problem: they were heavy.
This made them useless on rivers with rapids or waterfalls,
because they could not be carried round the obstacle. Boats made
from bark, fixed over wood frames, were much lighter, and easy to
carry overland. Called canoes, they were stitched together with
root fibres and sealed with tree resin.
Bark wasn't the only waterproof covering for boats. In the frozen
North, the Inuit stretched hide over slender wood frames to make
kayaks. Far to the south, hide-covered boats took a different shape:
Mississippi Indians' bullboats were circular, like a round pot or saucer.

▼ **Boats:** water was by far the quickest way to get around until
Europeans introduced the horse to North America. In their boats,
Indian people travelled for trade, to follow game, or for fishing.
Though small enough to navigate shallow streams, the boats
were also strong enough for long journeys on mighty rivers.

Northwestern dugout

**Northeastern
birchbark canoe**

Inuit kayak

Mississippi bullboat

In northern regions, slippery ice and snow made
journeys easier. A sledge enabled a dog team to
drag a heavy load – and even their owner – at some
speed. Light wooden sledges had simple suspension
systems made from rawhide straps. A coating of
frozen mud or moss on the runners made them
slide more easily. Some tribes, such as
the Micmac, did not use runners. Instead
they made sledges from flat strips of wood
curved up at the front. Their word for this
vehicle, *tobakun*, gave us the name by
which we know it today – toboggan.

Fearless Wolf is shocked and hurt
   To find that he's been raised by strangers.
He decides to start a journey
   Through the prairie's many dangers.
Wandering alone, he hopes
   He'll find his real family.
So he packs up food and clothing
   And takes his dog for company.

Medicine and Magic

The natural world provided Indian people with everything they needed for life – but it could also bring death and misery. No wonder they honoured animal and earth spirits, and respected anyone who could harness their power.

When a group of Koyukon Indians finished their meal of beaver meat, a young woman carried the bones to the river bank. Casting them into the water, she called out 'may you return next year'. These Alaskan Indians believed that the beaver was an important animal which deserved respect. They thought that unless they carried out this small ceremony, they would catch no more beavers.

Indian life was filled with rituals (special or sacred ways of doing things) like this one. Indian beliefs brought together what we would today call religion, magic and medicine. Though every different group had its own beliefs, ceremonies and rituals, there were some ideas that most shared.

▲ **Dancing:** for the Lakota (Sioux), as for other Native American people, dancing was an important way to conjure up spirits and to keep in touch with the supernatural.

Indian people did not separate real, natural things from supernatural things such as ghosts, spirits and gods. Things they could touch, smell, hunt and eat merged with magical things they imagined or saw in visions and dreams. The lives of the Indians depended on nature, so they thought of all natural things as powerful spirits that were either helpful allies or dangerous enemies. Whether good or evil, animal and plant spirits deserved honour and respect. In the Northwest, people believed that salmon were spirits that turned themselves into fish to help humans by being caught and eaten. The souls of the dead salmon travelled to the sea. There they waited for their bones to be thrown back into the river, so that they might be born again. To avoid

An avalanche of falling rocks
  Strikes Fearless Wolf upon the head.
A passing shaman, collecting roots,
  Finds him when he's almost dead.
The mystic man restores his health
  And gives him charms for his protection.
Then learning of his wandering quest,
  He points him in the right direction.

offending salmon spirits, Northwest Indians celebrated the first fish they caught each year with solemn offerings and speeches. Elsewhere on the continent, hunters used prayers, dreams, dances, songs and rituals to honour the animals they relied on for food. In areas where farming was more important than hunting, prayers to a corn god or sun god made sure crops grew well.

Magic and ceremony also played a big part in healing. Though Indian people were skilled at finding herbs that would cure disease and injury, they believed herbs alone were not powerful enough to heal serious illnesses.

◄ **Totem poles:**
Northwestern Indians carved these decorated marker posts from tree-trunks. Totem poles showed who owned a house, or welcomed strangers to a lakeside. They could also make fun of disgraced people, or hold the remains of the dead. Animals and spirits carved on the poles told a story, or showed to which family the pole belonged.

Dead and buried

Indians had a strong belief in the spirit world, so they perhaps feared death less than we do today. The families of the dead honoured them with simple funerals, then burned or buried the body, often with possessions or a favourite animal. In many places, including the Plains, tribes placed dead bodies on raised platforms or on scaffolds in trees, burying them when only bones remained.

Each tribe had its own ways of healing the sick, but most relied on members who had special magical abilities. *Shamans* got their powers directly from the spirit world; *priests* and *medicine men* learned from each other the skills and magic they needed for healing.

These people used their powers and knowledge in many other ways. They played an important part in religious ceremonies. Through visions and dreams they believed they could see into the future, and even control events that were yet to happen. Knowledge of plants helped them to do this: eating or smoking the right leaves or roots altered their minds, so that they could contact the world of powerful spirits. Ordinary people sometimes also used these herbal drugs. They took them to gain strength and courage; they shared them as a sign of friendship; and they used some – such as tobacco – both in ceremonies and rituals, and for enjoyment.

20

Smoke Signals

Though they had no written language, American Indians had many other ways of communicating. Hand signs bridged language gaps between tribes. Runners and hill-top fire or smoke beacons sent signals over long distances.

Native American peoples used a bewildering variety of languages: some 400, possibly more, across the whole continent. Most were as different as French is from English. In California alone people used 20 different languages: more than in all Europe. Today at least half of the Indian languages are 'extinct' – nobody uses or understands them – and most of the rest are spoken only by a few old people. There are some important exceptions, like the Cherokee, Choctaw, Cree, Hopi, Navajo, Ojibwa, Taos and Zuni languages that are still spoken by many people, both adults and children.

▲ **Winter counts:** the small pictures (pictographs) of this Indian calendar recorded famines, victories in war, successful hunts, smallpox epidemics and other important events. With its help, the keeper of the winter count could remember and pass on the tribe's history.

Clearly communication between Indians who did not speak the same language was difficult. On the Plains, sign language helped. The Arapahoe, Blackfoot, Cheyenne, Sioux, and some other tribes signed to each other as people with hearing or speech difficulties do today. Many signs were like mime (a play without speech). For example, the sign for a hatchet was to grip the right elbow with the left hand, and make a chopping action with the right hand held straight like an axe blade.

Native Americans did not record their languages with a written alphabet, though some northern tribes did keep a written history in the form of a *winter count* – a kind of calendar. Painted on to a buffalo skin, this recorded the single most important event of the past year with a small picture or sign. When asked their age, members of the tribe often referred to the sign painted for the year of their birth.

Without a written language, Indians passed on their history in speech, rhyme and song. However, at least one Indian believed his tribe would be more powerful if they could write. Sequoyah (1770–1843) devised a way of writing the sounds of his Cherokee people. Thanks to the *syllabary* (speech sound list) he invented in 1821, most of the Cherokee people quickly learned to read and write. Today, linguists (people who study language) write down the sounds of Cherokee and other Indian languages with their own phonetic (speech-sound) alphabet.

For long-distance communication, Indian people relied on runners and smoke or fire beacons. Until European settlers introduced horses to the continent, runners carried urgent messages on foot, sometimes over long distances. Though any fit and healthy Indian might act as a runner, some tribes had special runners who did no other job. In central California, for example, Nomlaki 'newsboys' rushed messages 100 km (60 miles) or more.

Smoke signals, made famous by Hollywood movies, were widely used only in the western

▲ **History in speech:** Indians did not write because they did not need to. Story telling, songs and rhymes kept their knowledge alive.

Plains. There the flat landscape made them visible up to 80 km (50 miles) away. Damp leaves thrown on a fire created the smoke, and the choice of plant could change the colour. A blanket thrown over the fire and removed produced 'puffs'. Codes of puffs were arranged in advance, but there were a few standard messages: one puff meant 'attention'; two signalled 'all clear' and three was a warning.

Navajo Language in the Second World War

Indian language helped the USA defeat its Japanese foe in the Second World War (1939–45). By 1942, the Japanese had broken American codes and could understand every order broadcast by radio. So the US army recruited several hundred Navajo radio operators. Their language baffled the enemy listening in, and kept communications secret.

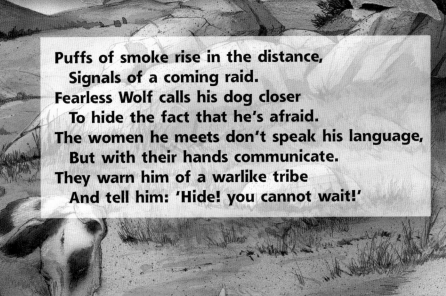

Puffs of smoke rise in the distance,
  Signals of a coming raid.
Fearless Wolf calls his dog closer
  To hide the fact that he's afraid.
The women he meets don't speak his language,
  But with their hands communicate.
They warn him of a warlike tribe
  And tell him: 'Hide! you cannot wait!'

On the Warpath

For a young Plains warrior, joining a raiding party was a dangerous but exciting route to success. Capturing scalps or just touching the enemy were traditional ways to earn respect, wealth, and even a beautiful bride.

An Indian raid was a terrifying experience. Creeping out of the dawn mist, the warriors aimed to take their victims by surprise. Their painted faces and buffalo-horn head-dresses gave them a frightening appearance. They fought fiercely, and would rather die than retreat. Their weapons were simple but deadly: short bows and wooden clubs tipped with stone. The small, flimsy shields they carried would hardly stop an arrow. However, the warriors believed the magic signs painted on the shields protected them better than the double-thickness hide shirts they wore as armour.

The Indian tribes the raiders attacked were traditional enemies. Often raids were in revenge for an earlier defeat, perhaps many years before. Successful

◄ **Invisible armour:** compared to a modern soldier or a medieval knight, an Indian going to war had few defences. Yet to the warrior, a magic charm such as a bear-claw necklace gave as much protection as a suit of steel armour.

raiders returned home with grisly trophies, such as the fingers or scalps of the people they had killed. These weren't just for show. Taking someone's scalp made them your slave in the spirit life that followed death. Scalps were not the biggest prize, however. Greater honour went to the warriors who had managed to touch their foes in the battle – with their hands, with a bow, or with a special 'coup-stick'. Each touch was called a 'coup', and they were counted in a strict scoring system.

Warriors who counted many coups were rewarded not only with respect in their tribe, but also with special clothes,

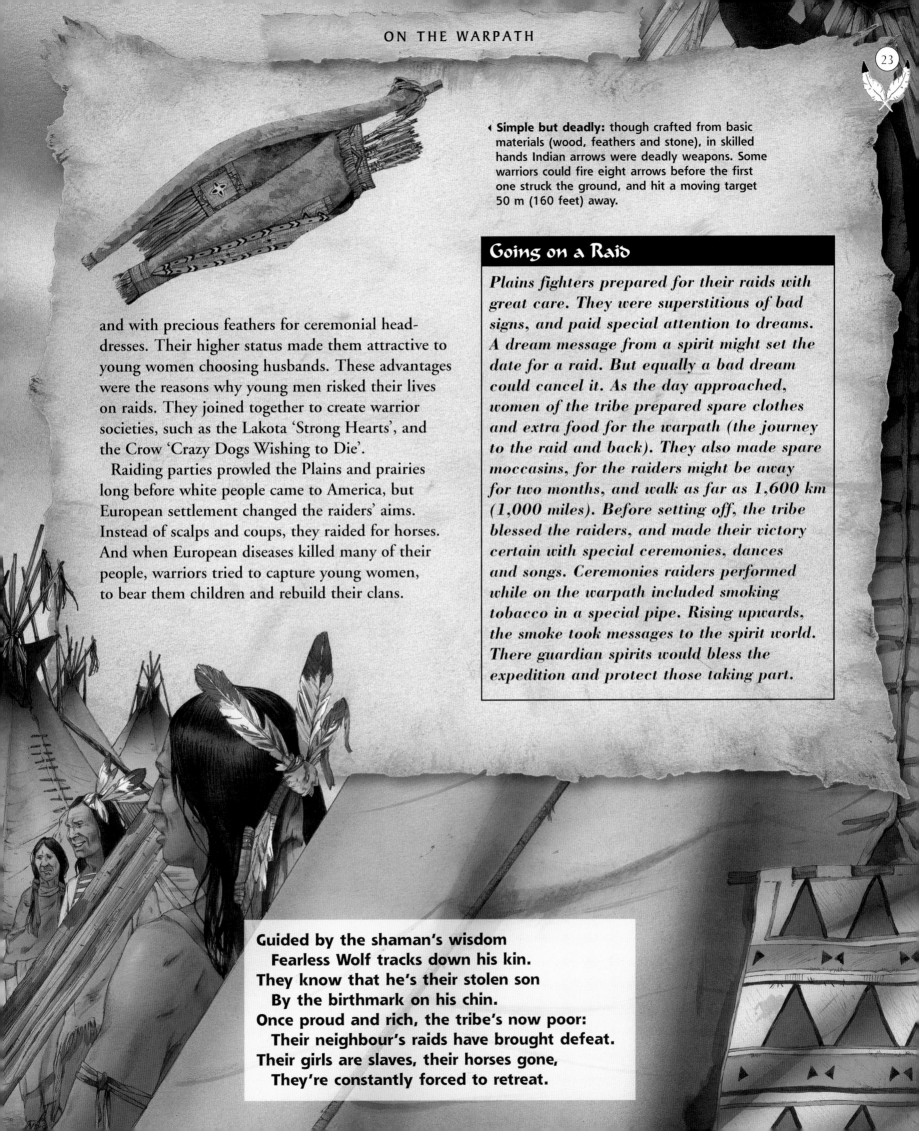

◀ **Simple but deadly:** though crafted from basic materials (wood, feathers and stone), in skilled hands Indian arrows were deadly weapons. Some warriors could fire eight arrows before the first one struck the ground, and hit a moving target 50 m (160 feet) away.

and with precious feathers for ceremonial head-dresses. Their higher status made them attractive to young women choosing husbands. These advantages were the reasons why young men risked their lives on raids. They joined together to create warrior societies, such as the Lakota 'Strong Hearts', and the Crow 'Crazy Dogs Wishing to Die'.

Raiding parties prowled the Plains and prairies long before white people came to America, but European settlement changed the raiders' aims. Instead of scalps and coups, they raided for horses. And when European diseases killed many of their people, warriors tried to capture young women, to bear them children and rebuild their clans.

Going on a Raid

Plains fighters prepared for their raids with great care. They were superstitious of bad signs, and paid special attention to dreams. A dream message from a spirit might set the date for a raid. But equally a bad dream could cancel it. As the day approached, women of the tribe prepared spare clothes and extra food for the warpath (the journey to the raid and back). They also made spare moccasins, for the raiders might be away for two months, and walk as far as 1,600 km (1,000 miles). Before setting off, the tribe blessed the raiders, and made their victory certain with special ceremonies, dances and songs. Ceremonies raiders performed while on the warpath included smoking tobacco in a special pipe. Rising upwards, the smoke took messages to the spirit world. There guardian spirits would bless the expedition and protect those taking part.

Guided by the shaman's wisdom
  Fearless Wolf tracks down his kin.
They know that he's their stolen son
  By the birthmark on his chin.
Once proud and rich, the tribe's now poor:
  Their neighbour's raids have brought defeat.
Their girls are slaves, their horses gone,
  They're constantly forced to retreat.

European Invaders

When Europeans began crossing the Atlantic, the lives of Native North Americans changed forever. The white-faced people stole the Indians' land; they laughed at their stone-age weapons; and they left them dying of strange new diseases.

Europeans knew almost nothing about North America and its people until 1513, when a Spanish expedition landed in Florida. Over the next century many more adventurers arrived, in search of gold, and of a northern sea route linking the Atlantic and Pacific Oceans. Spaniards sailed to the American mainland from their Caribbean island base of Cuba, or marched overland from Mexico. People from other European nations soon rivalled the Spanish in the search for riches. By the seventeenth century, French fur traders had begun exploring what

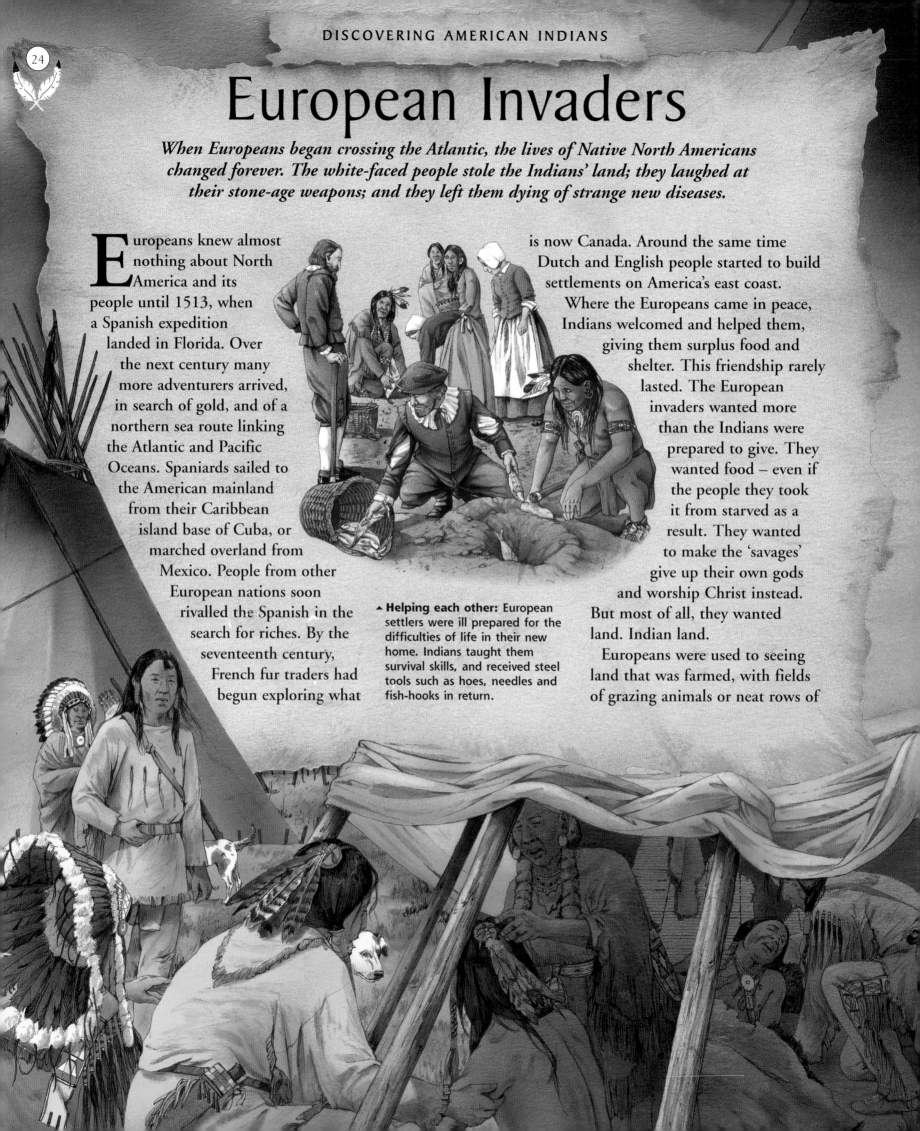

▲ **Helping each other:** European settlers were ill prepared for the difficulties of life in their new home. Indians taught them survival skills, and received steel tools such as hoes, needles and fish-hooks in return.

is now Canada. Around the same time Dutch and English people started to build settlements on America's east coast.

Where the Europeans came in peace, Indians welcomed and helped them, giving them surplus food and shelter. This friendship rarely lasted. The European invaders wanted more than the Indians were prepared to give. They wanted food – even if the people they took it from starved as a result. They wanted to make the 'savages' give up their own gods and worship Christ instead. But most of all, they wanted land. Indian land.

Europeans were used to seeing land that was farmed, with fields of grazing animals or neat rows of ripe crops. They saw the Indian lands as 'wilderness', unfenced and unfarmed. The European settlers took the land as their own, driving off or enslaving its Indian inhabitants, often with brutal force.

As white settlers spread out west from America's east coast, Indian people fought to stop the theft of their land. In 1763 the English tried to make a deal that would end the attacks threatening their settlers. They promised Indian people that they would only take land to the east of the Appalachian mountains. But as more settlers arrived, hungry for more land, Indians were again driven back, to the Mississippi river and beyond.

European exploration eventually opened up the whole continent to settlers. Indians everywhere were forced from the best land. Farmers claimed huge areas for raising cattle. When gold was discovered in California in 1850 huge numbers of would-be gold-miners trekked west – straight through Indian country.

◄ **Sabotage:** Indians saw railroads as yet another threat to their hunting. They ambushed and burned trains. They also attacked the construction gangs laying the rails.

Later, railroads cut through traditional tribal lands. Indian resistance was violent, but hopeless, for European settlers had many advantages. Their numbers were growing, and their guns were much more powerful weapons than the Indians' bows, axes and spears. They also had an invisible ally: disease. European people brought with them diseases which were previously unknown in America. Indians had no natural resistance to them, and died of infections from which Europeans quickly recovered. Diseases such as smallpox killed one in ten of its victims in Europe. In North America, it wiped out nine out of every ten Indians who caught it. Many more died of measles and 'flu. The Europeans first fought the Indians with guns, but eventually defeated them with disease.

The tribe is sick: they've caught a fever
    From white men keen to take their land.
The braves are too weak to resist:
    The settlers get what they demand.
Fearless Wolf can see that soon
    The tribe will lose their ancient freedom.
To beat the settlers, they must fight
    And he will be the one to lead them.

Horses and Guns

Horseback hunters armed with guns are everyone's idea of what Indians were like.
But this lifestyle did not last long, and it only became possible when European settlers
had introduced a new weapon and a new form of transport.

Though native horses once roamed North America's grasslands, they died out some 9,000 years ago. The first horses that Indians saw were those introduced by Spanish explorers in the early sixteenth century.

Indians in the Southwest looked after these horses and became expert riders and trainers. Using traded, stolen and strayed horses, they built up herds of their own. Knowledge and ownership of horses gradually spread north and east from Mexico.

Horses made a big difference. Riding was much faster than walking, and horses could carry heavy

▲ **Expert riders:** constant practice made Plains Indians expert horsemen. They could aim and fire with deadly accuracy while riding at full gallop. This skill made them dangerous enemies for white settlers even before guns replaced their bows.

loads. Tribes that owned horses had an advantage over those that did not. Horses changed things within tribes and clans, too. They were a form of wealth, and a sign that their owners were important.

The region most affected by the introduction of the horse was the Plains. All Plains tribes had horses by the early nineteenth century. They used them to hunt buffalo, training their mounts in the special skills needed to run down the heavy beasts. Buffalo horses became especially prized, but all horses were valuable. Horse raids, which aimed to steal horses from rival clans, brought a new kind of war to Indian life.

Horses made travel easier, and some village-dwelling people gave up their settled lifestyle. Instead, they wandered the Plains, following the vast buffalo herds which they hunted for meat and skins (*see page* 11).

Contact with English and French settlers also introduced Indians to guns. Seeing their families and companions killed by rifles and handguns made them realize the power of these weapons. At first guns had little real value to Indians. They were useless for hunting because they made buffalo stampede. They were not as easy as bows to load and fire from horseback. However, as they got more guns and ammunition, Indians began to use them in wars with rival tribes. Well-armed groups could fight off attacks from enemies armed with traditional weapons.

The arrival of the horse and the gun together changed life on the Plains completely. It led to what we now think of as a typical Indian: a horseback buffalo hunter, armed with a gun. This way of life did not last long, however, for the gun had another effect. White people had far more guns than Indians. And for the newcomers, hunting buffalo was not a way of life, but a form of entertainment. This difference was soon to help seal the fate of the Indian people of the Plains.

Trading nations

To get guns and other manufactured goods from white people, Indians traded. For centuries they had hunted and trapped game for their skins. Now they could swap beaver and buffalo for guns, metal pots and tools, glass beads, fabric, brandy and tobacco.

▶ **Trading:** Indians did not use or understand money, and at first had little idea of the value of what they were trading. Dishonest white merchants often cheated them.

By trading skins of buffalo
    He gets some guns, and arms his braves,
Rescues all their stolen horses
    And the girls who've lived as slaves.
With some help from friendly tribes
    Fearless Wolf mounts his attack
But as they're driven from the land
    The settlers shout out: 'We'll be back!'

Reservations

Cheated out of their land or driven off by settlers' bullets, Indians retreated to reservations – small areas set aside for them. Their way of life was not safe even there, for white hunters destroyed the buffalo on which they depended.

When white Americans won their independence in the Revolutionary War of 1776–83, they defeated not only the British, but Native Americans too. Few Indians had actually fought on the British side, but white Americans felt that their victory in the war gave them freedom to take Indian lands.

To make this legal, the American government made treaties (agreements) with Indian tribes. Starting in 1778, they persuaded Indian leaders to give away their land in exchange for money, food, education and protection. The treaties reserved land for Indian use, but these 'reservations' were smaller or less valuable than the tribal lands taken from the Indians. For example, the 1795 Treaty of Greenville aimed to bring peace to the Northwest. In it Indians signed away 'land at the mouth of the Chicago River, emptying into . . . lake Michigan'. The city of Chicago now stands there. The treaty reserved

◄ **Reservations:** for the Indians forced into them, reservations were like prisons. They could not continue their traditional ways of life, and had to survive on government hand-outs.

land for the Indians, but settlers soon overran it. By 1812, not one Indian was left in the area.

Officials obtained other treaties by cheating. Where no one leader spoke for a whole tribe, officials simply made the most helpful man a 'paper chief'. They showed how to 'touch the pen' next to his name on a treaty he could not read. Officials got Indian leaders drunk, made them sign at gunpoint, or simply forged the treaty.

Treaties weren't the only way to move Indians off their land. New laws helped, too. The Indian Removal act of 1830 forced Cherokees, Creeks, Choctaws, Chickasaws and Seminoles off their

The victory was easily won,
    But the settlers' threat comes true.
When they return, it's with the army:
    A long, long line of men in blue.
A rifle shot hits Fearless Wolf —
    He's buried in an unmarked grave.
His people move to reservations
    But don't forget their warrior brave.

Custer's Last Stand

In the Plains Indian War, Native Americans fought settlers and the US army from the 1840s to the 1880s. Sometimes, the Indians won major victories. In 1876, at Little Bighorn, Montana, Sioux and Cheyenne warriors surrounded and wiped out a cavalry force led by Lieutenant Colonel George Custer (right). More often the Indians could not stand up to the better organized and armed soldiers. Final defeat came with the massacre of Wounded Knee, South Dakota, in 1890. There, the US cavalry killed nearly 300 Sioux, mostly women and children who were trying to reach Red Cloud Agency on Pine Ridge Reservation. Their chief, Sitting Bull, had been killed two weeks earlier on his Standing Rock Reservation.

traditional lands to worse land far to the west. The US army marched 100,000 of them from their villages. Many had to be chained up to force them to leave, and a quarter – 25,000 people – died on the journey. Forced removals such as this led to over 40 years of open warfare, called the Plains Indian War. The Indians were eventually defeated (*see box above*).

While Indians were being defeated in battle and cheated out of their land, white hunters were shooting the buffalo on which they relied. Hunters shot buffalo first for hides and meat, but then later just for the pleasure of killing. Indian reservations were out of bounds to hunters, but they waited

outside, by the few waterholes, and slaughtered animals that came from the reservation to drink.

With their land and food gone, and their people dying from imported diseases, Indian numbers fell quickly. Before contact with white people, there were thought to be 4–8 million Native North Americans. By 1900, only 400,000 remained.

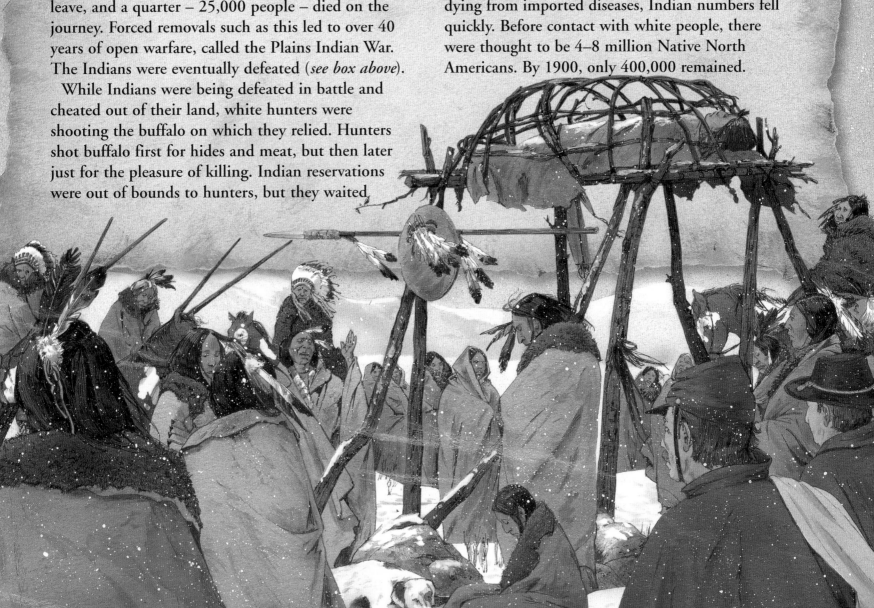

Looking to the Future

Attacks on Indians didn't end with their defeat at Wounded Knee. American laws carried on punishing them. But Indians fought for their human rights, and today their traditions get the respect they deserve.

Once a tough, proud, free people, Native Americans were bullied and hunted at the start of the twentieth century. Crammed in reservations where there was little work, families were forced to rely on government aid. Despair made many Indians heavy drinkers.

The American Government had always hoped Indian people would give up their traditions and merge with white society. To 'help' them, officials split up families, sending children to boarding schools and forcing them to speak English. They split up reservations into small plots, each big enough for one family to farm. But it was not just land and families that the government was dividing. Their real aim was to destroy Indian tribes and culture. US President Teddy Roosevelt called the law to divide reservations 'a mighty pulverizing (smashing) engine to break up the tribal mass'.

It almost worked. Indian people found it difficult to protect their way of life. This is hardly surprising: they were not a single people, but 500 different nations. Their languages did not even have a word that meant the same as 'Indian'.

In 1924, Indians were at last made citizens of the United States, but this did little to help them. The US government still failed to respect Indian rights. They began to 'terminate' tribes in the 1950s, ending government aid, and removing the tribes' rights to make their own laws.

Things improved in the 1960s with the rise of the civil rights movement which aimed to

▼ **Crafts:** tribal designs like these are still very popular, but today's artists and craft workers don't all cling to traditional styles. Some use their background as a starting point, and create much more modern works.

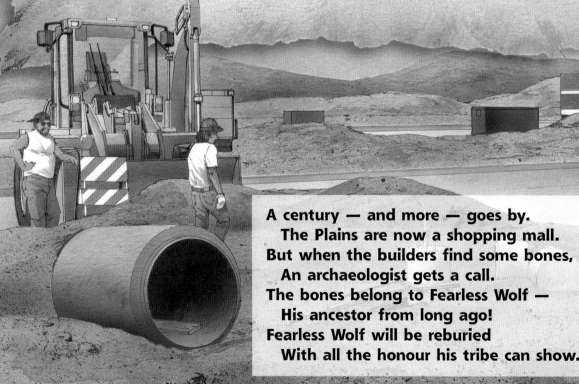

A century — and more — goes by.
  The Plains are now a shopping mall.
But when the builders find some bones,
  An archaeologist gets a call.
The bones belong to Fearless Wolf —
  His ancestor from long ago!
Fearless Wolf will be reburied
  With all the honour his tribe can show.

make black and white Americans equal. As part of the movement, Indians began to fight for *their* human rights. In 1969, protesting Indians took over San Francisco's abandoned Alcatraz prison. Four years later, Sioux people occupied the site of the Wounded Knee massacre (*see page* 29). Thanks to these and other protests, the government passed laws to protect Indians and their traditions, religion, and way of life. The new laws also gave them more power to govern themselves.

With changes in the law came changes in the way Native American people saw themselves. Growing Indian pride led more people of mixed race to respect their Indian ancestors. Training as archaeologists, Indians literally dug up their background and culture.

Progress brought wealth, too. On some reservations, bingo became a boom industry. White Americans flocked to gamble for big money prizes. Indians also made money from white tourists' growing interest in anything Indian.

However, reservation life is just one part of the modern Native American world. Many Indians now have homes in towns. More live in New York and Los Angeles than anywhere else in the USA. Whether on the reservation or in the big city, Indian people are rediscovering their roots. They're creating music and art that returns to the traditions of their ancestors: there's even a Grammy award for Native American music.

◄ **Patchwork quilts:** still in use today, the 'Morning Star' is one of the oldest Native American patterns used in patchwork. It represents the planet Venus.

▼ **Archaeology:** when builders dig foundations, they must employ archaeologists to record any Indian remains they find. A few younger Native Americans do this work, but it's not popular with older people, who fear disturbing their ancestor's souls.

Index